WAKE UP!

NO MORE EXCUSES

VAR FRAMTID

CHOOL STRIKE FOR CLIMATE

FRIDAYS FOR FUTURE

HUELGA ESCOLAR POR EL CLIMA

STOP BIOCIDO

there is no planet B

기후변화 문제에 대한 결석시위

ÖKO STATT EGO

SCIENCE NOT SILENCE

Little People, **BIG DREAMS®**
GRETA THUNBERG

Written by
Maria Isabel Sánchez Vegara

Illustrated by
Anke Weckmann

Frances Lincoln
Children's Books

Greta was a little Swedish girl who learnt from her parents to turn off the lights, not to waste water and never throw out food: three simple lessons for being kind to nature that most grown-ups haven't quite learnt yet.

She was very proud of her great-grand-uncle Svante, a brilliant scientist who – a hundred years before Greta was born – made an alarming discovery: the planet was warming up and humans were the ones responsible for it.

But even though adults have known this for a long time, not much has been done to change it. Every day, millions of tonnes of toxic gases are thrown into the air. Greta wondered what would be left of the planet when she grew up.

At school, she watched a film about climate change. Most students were worried about polar bears losing their homes because of the North Pole melting but, once the film was over, everyone forgot about it. Everyone... except Greta.

She felt so hopeless about the future that she stopped talking. Doctors said she had selective mutism and Asperger's syndrome, which meant she would only speak and pay attention to what was really important to her.

Some may have thought that these were two terrible conditions, but they ended up becoming Greta's greatest powers. They helped her to stick to her promise: to do everything she could to slow down the planet's warming.

Greta started by convincing her parents to give up air travel and stop eating meat. But there were dozens of other little things she could do! She knew that she couldn't stand up for something without walking the walk.

She had done her homework, but it wasn't enough. To stop global warming, politicians had to do theirs, too.

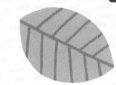

SKOLSTREJK FÖR KLIMATET

One day, instead of going to school, Greta decided to sit quietly in front of the Swedish Parliament with a sign.

Not very many people noticed her that first day, but it didn't bother Greta. She kept going with her strike every single Friday, and every time she got there, more and more students joined her.

It was time for children to wake up the adults!
Soon, all over the world, thousands of students started
skipping school to protest outside of their city halls,
fighting for the future of the next generation.

Inspired by Greta's story, millions of people – from Melbourne to San Francisco – flooded the streets in the first world strike against global warming. It was the biggest environmental protest ever!

She crossed the ocean on a wind and solar-powered boat to speak in front of world leaders. In the name of all children, Greta asked people in power to stop making up excuses and start acting before it's too late.

What started with just one girl with a handmade sign became a movement that includes us all. Because global warming is the greatest challenge humanity will ever face, but little Greta is no longer alone.

GRETA THUNBERG

(Born 2003)

2018   2019

Greta Thunberg was born in Stockholm, Sweden, in 2003. When she was
eight years old, she learned that human activity was causing the Earth
to become hotter and hotter, causing a climate crisis. This could result in
animal and plant species going extinct, as well as more natural disasters
like floods and hurricanes. Greta could not understand why more people
did not take climate change seriously. No one in power was doing much
to solve the problem. This made Greta depressed, but she did what she
could to make a difference. She stopped using aeroplanes to travel and
became vegan. But she knew she would have to do more to make people
realise the danger of climate change. When she was 15, she began missing
school to protest outside the Swedish Parliament. Other children soon joined

2020   2020

her 'School Strike for Climate', first in Sweden, then across the world. This forced governments to take notice of her cause. Greta was invited to speak to world leaders and activists. She became known for telling the truth when no one else would. When she was just 16, Greta told leaders of the United Nations that they were destroying her generation's future by ignoring climate change. Millions of people around the world were inspired by Greta to take action wherever they could. Some powerful people have said that she is too young to be worth listening to. But Greta knows better. She called Asperger's syndrome her superpower, as it allows her to fight for what she knows is right without worrying about her critics. Today, Greta continues to stand up for the environment, and is seen as a symbol of hope for a cleaner, greener future.

Want to find out more about **Greta Thunberg?**

Have a read of these great books:

No One Is Too Small to Make a Difference by Greta Thunberg

Greta and the Giants: inspired by Greta Thunberg's stand to save the world

by Zoë Tucker and Zoe Persico

Brimming with creative inspiration, how-to projects, and useful information to enrich your everyday life, Quarto Knows is a favourite destination for those pursuing their interests and passions. Visit our site and dig deeper with our books into your area of interest: Quarto Creates, Quarto Cooks, Quarto Homes, Quarto Lives, Quarto Drives, Quarto Explores, Quarto Gifts, or Quarto Kids.

Text copyright © 2020 Maria Isabel Sanchez Vegara. Illustrations copyright © 2020 Anke Weckmann.

Original concept of the series by Maria Isabel Sánchez Vegara, published by Alba Editorial, s.l.u

Produced under trademark licence from Alba Editorial s.l.u and Beautifool Couple S.L.

First Published in the UK in 2020 by Frances Lincoln Children's Books, an imprint of The Quarto Group.

The Old Brewery, 6 Blundell Street, London N7 9BH, United Kingdom.

T 020 7700 6700 **www.QuartoKnows.com**

Series first published in Spain in 2020 under the title Pequeña & Grande by Alba Editorial, s.l.u., Baixada de Sant Miquel, 1, 08002 Barcelona. www.albaeditorial.es

All rights reserved.

Published by arrangement with Alba Editorial, s.l.u.

ISBN 978-0-7112-5643-9
eISBN 978-0-7112-5646-0

Set in Futura BT.

Published by Katie Cotton • Designed by Karissa Santos

Edited by Katy Flint • Production by Caragh McAleenan

Manufactured in Guangdong, China CC092020

3 5 7 9 8 4 6

Photographic acknowledgements (pages 28-29, from left to right) 1. Greta Thunberg leads a school strike and sits outside of Riksdagen, the Swedish parliament building for climate change on August 28, 2018 in Stockholm © Jasper Chamber / Alamy Stock Photo 2. WASHINGTON, DC - SEPTEMBER 13: Teenage Swedish climate activist Greta Thunberg delivers brief remarks surrounded by other student environmental advocates during a strike to demand action be taken on climate change outside the White House on September 13, 2019 in Washington, DC. © Sarah Silbiger / Getty Images. 3. Climate activists Greta Thunberg, centre, Vanessa Nakate, centre right, Isabelle Axelsson, bottom third left, and Luisa Neubauer, centre left, hold placards while taking part in a demonstration on the closing day of the World Economic Forum (WEF) in Davos, Switzerland, on Friday, Jan. 24, 2020. © Simon Dawson/Bloomberg via Getty Images 4. Swedish climate activist Greta Thunberg poses for media as she arrives for a news conference in Davos, Switzerland, 2020. © Markus Schreiber/AP/Shutterstock.

Collect the
Little People, **BIG DREAMS**® series:

FRIDA KAHLO	**COCO CHANEL**	**MAYA ANGELOU**	**AMELIA EARHART**	**AGATHA CHRISTIE**	**MARIE CURIE**

ISBN: 978-1-84780-770-0   ISBN: 978-1-84780-771-7   ISBN: 978-1-84780-890-5   ISBN: 978-1-84780-885-1   ISBN: 978-1-84780-959-9   ISBN: 978-1-84780-961-2

ROSA PARKS	**AUDREY HEPBURN**	**EMMELINE PANKHURST**	**ELLA FITZGERALD**	**ADA LOVELACE**	**JANE AUSTEN**

ISBN: 978-1-78603-017-7   ISBN: 978-1-78603-052-8   ISBN: 978-1-78603-019-1   ISBN: 978-1-78603-086-3   ISBN: 978-1-78603-075-7   ISBN: 978-1-78603-119-8

GEORGIA O'KEEFFE	**HARRIET TUBMAN**	**ANNE FRANK**	**MOTHER TERESA**	**JOSEPHINE BAKER**	**L. M. MONTGOMERY**

ISBN: 978-1-78603-121-1   ISBN: 978-1-78603-289-8   ISBN: 978-1-78603-292-8   ISBN: 978-1-78603-290-4   ISBN: 978-1-78603-291-1   ISBN: 978-1-78603-295-9

JANE GOODALL	**SIMONE DE BEAUVOIR**	**MUHAMMAD ALI**	**STEPHEN HAWKING**	**MARIA MONTESSORI**	**VIVIENNE WESTWOOD**

ISBN: 978-1-78603-294-2   ISBN: 978-1-78603-293-5   ISBN: 978-1-78603-733-6   ISBN: 978-1-78603-732-9   ISBN: 978-1-78603-753-4   ISBN: 978-1-78603-756-5

MAHATMA GANDHI	**DAVID BOWIE**	**WILMA RUDOLPH**	**DOLLY PARTON**	**BRUCE LEE**	**RUDOLF NUREYEV**

ISBN: 978-1-78603-334-5   ISBN: 978-1-78603-803-6   ISBN: 978-1-78603-750-3   ISBN: 978-1-78603-759-6   ISBN: 978-1-78603-335-2   ISBN: 978-1-78603-336-9

ZAHA HADID

ISBN: 978-1-78603-744-2

MARY SHELLEY

ISBN: 978-1-78603-747-3

MARTIN LUTHER KING JR.

ISBN: 978-0-7112-4566-2

DAVID ATTENBOROUGH

ISBN: 978-0-7112-4563-1

ASTRID LINDGREN

ISBN: 978-1-78603-762-6

EVONNE GOOLAGONG

ISBN: 978-0-7112-4585-3

BOB DYLAN

ISBN: 978-0-7112-4674-4

ALAN TURING

ISBN: 978-0-7112-4677-5

BILLIE JEAN KING

ISBN: 978-0-7112-4692-8

GRETA THUNBERG

ISBN: 978-0-7112-5643-9

JESSE OWENS

ISBN: 978-0-7112-4582-2

JEAN-MICHEL BASQUIAT

ISBN: 978-0-7112-4579-2

ARETHA FRANKLIN

ISBN: 978-0-7112-4687-4

CORAZON AQUINO

ISBN: 978-0-7112-4683-6

PELÉ

ISBN: 978-0-7112-4574-7

ERNEST SHACKLETON

ISBN: 978-0-7112-4570-9

STEVE JOBS

ISBN: 978-0-7112-4576-1

AYRTON SENNA

ISBN: 978-0-7112-4671-3

LOUISE BOURGEOIS

ISBN: 978-0-7112-4689-8

ELTON JOHN

ISBN: 978-0-7112-5838-9

JOHN LENNON

ISBN: 978-0-7112-5765-8

PRINCE

ISBN: 978-0-7112-5437-4

CHARLES DARWIN

ISBN: 978-0-7112-5769-6

CAPTAIN TOM MOORE

ISBN: 978-0-7112-6207-2

HANS CHRISTIAN ANDERSEN

ISBN: 978-0-7112-5932-4

ACTIVITY BOOKS

STICKER ACTIVITY BOOK

ISBN: 978-0-7112-6011-5

COLOURING BOOK

ISBN: 978-0-7112-6135-8

LITTLE ME, BIG DREAMS JOURNAL

ISBN: 978-0-7112-4888-5